The Key Is Me

Treasures of the Heart

Inspirational Poetry

By

C. J. Lovell

Illustrations by Dana Sitarzewski

C. J. Lovell
P. O. Box 40515
Phoenix, AZ 85067
www.cjlovell.com

Printed in the United States of America
First Printing April 2009
ISBN: 978-0-578-01854-6
C. J. Lovell

Cover Design and Typesetting: C. J. Lovell
Editing: Joan Branin
Graphics: Dana Sitarzewski / Jaguar Woman Web Design
www.jaguarwoman.com

Dedicated To

Michael, J. Michael, Craig,
Carson, Joanie and
Ms. Purrfect Purr
1994 - 2009

Author's Note

I'm a fortunate person who is very blessed and loved. My childhood friend Joanie has always told me I had the gift to write and I should one day write a book.

I have always believed in My Heavenly Father, but it was during difficult times and soul searching, that I turned to Him asking for spiritual guidance. I learned how much He loves me and He is always there by my side.

I also learned about my personal angels and their love for me. If I quiet myself and listen carefully, I can hear them guiding me every step of the way. It was then I started writing poetry and meditations revealing the wonderful inspiration of my angels. They would use my writings as a means of guiding and teaching me, helping me to find my path to happiness and inner peace.

As I became more in tune with my Heavenly Father and my soul began to stir with an abundance of inspiration. I started to write more and more. With each poem I began to understand how important it is to change my thoughts towards only what I wanted to manifest in my life.

I know my Heavenly Father and my angels have inspired me to pass on what I have learned. My hope is my poems will be an inspiration to you, lighting your path to happiness and inner peace. Each of us is very special, each of us is unique and each of us is loved by our Heavenly Father and our very own special angels. It is my prayer my works will help you to learn who you really are, realizing you can become whatever your mind can conceive.

My prayers are with you always.

Beginning of a New Day

"This is the beginning of a new day.

I have been given this day to use as I will. I can waste it, or use it.

I can make it a day long to be remembered for its joy, its beauty and its achievements, or it can be filled with pettiness.

What I do today is important because I am exchanging a day of my life for it.

When tomorrow comes this day will be gone forever, but I shall hold something which I have traded for it.

It may be no more than a memory, but if it is a worthy one I shall not regret the price.

I want it to be gain not loss, good not evil, success not failure."
Author Unknown

"We are each of us angels with only one wing and we can only fly by embracing one another" *Luciano de Crescenzo*

"As human beings, our greatness lays not so much in being able to remake the world... as in being able to remake ourselves."
Mahatma Gandhi

Table of Contents

The Key Is Me

The Key Is Me

Oh, my precious soul, where the blackness of discontentment lurks, if only the sun would brightly shine.

The torments and unrest of all the world's troubles are on my shoulders alone.

The heaviness and pain of each dark cloud, no doubt was given to me by design.

Never a positive thought do I have; continually all I do is moan and groan.

I watch all God's splendor pass me by, never once believing I could fly.

In the security of my own self-imposed prison; not seeing a way to flee; just on the verge of breaking down.

Appalling fear and self-doubt are destroying my soul; you see I have given up and won't even try.

Hiding my shame of depression and self-hatred, I wear the painted face of a clown.

Never, never once did it cross my mind, not even once... never once did I realize I could truly fly.

The strength of my doubting thoughts and the demons of my past keep me from walking through God's lighted door.

Never, never once did it cross my mind, not even once... never once did I believe I could soar through the awesome blue sky.

Just like the turn of a key or the turn of a knob... just as easy as that I made my life so much more.

For me, a new life began with just a positive thought or two, then my thoughts grew into three or four, then there were more and more; so many I can no longer count.

By simply changing my thinking my mind grew into a beautiful garden, and it all started with just one positive seed.

The yearning of dreams unfulfilled; now wonderfully put in front of me; each day, right before my eyes, I watch my blessings continue to mount.

All the burdens of my self-inflected pain and self-denial, always saying, "I can't," from this prison I have been freed.

I now stand on a mountaintop with my head way above the clouds; there is no doubt the beautiful golden rays of the sun will always shine down on me; all that is required of me is to simply try.

So many dreams in my life I have the desire to achieve, at last I have the key, and finally I realize they all must start inside of me.

All I have to do is want to fly bad enough; believing in myself, all I have to do is spread my wondrous wings and sail way up high in the sky.

Belief in myself, never doubting for a second, planting seeds of flowers; these are the keys, now my happiness and inner peace is a guarantee.

The key is me...

The key is me...

I Want To Be a Soft Person

I Want To Be a Soft Person

My view for this brief moment in time...

I have decided I want only soft people in my life. Soft people are those who are, well, "SOFT".

Soft people are loving, kind, empathetic, caring, understanding, giving and a little spiritual. Soft people see their own inner beauty, and they help those around them see their inner beauty.

The people they are around leave feeling good about themselves. I remember a quote I once read that I thought was very profound, of which I will always remember because it is so true.

"People do not remember what you did for them,
but they remember how you made them feel."

Have you ever said, "Well, I don't like so and so." It is not so much that we dislike so and so, but it is a matter of how we feel about ourselves when we are around those who we feel we do not like.

We always like and enjoy being around people where we feel comfortable and good about ourselves. We like those people and we like being around them, looking forward to spending more time with them.   When we are with them we like ourselves.

If we feel negative in any way about ourselves when we are around certain people; in actuality we are feeling dislike towards ourselves. We are uncomfortable and then we think or say; "I don't like so and so."

I believe people become soft when they have had difficult times, been hurt and had to pick themselves up by the boot straps, hanging in there and never giving up. Of course, there are always exceptions and certainly not the only criteria to becoming a soft person.

After much self reflection they eventually learn to love and respect themselves in a healthy way. They begin to see the beauty of who they are, then reflecting it back to everyone they meet. Others feel this wonderful soft energy and want more of it.

I also believe there are special souls in this world, who are born knowing their inner beauty and never lose sight of it. These people are the angels in our lives.

For the most part though, unless you know firsthand what difficult times are or have felt pain, it is much more difficult to have empathy than it is for those who have.

Sadly, there are some people who never become soft. They haven't gone through experiences that allow them to see what hurt and difficult times are like. They lack understanding, becoming hard and opinionated, unable to have empathy towards others.

There are also those who have been hurt and had to face difficult times in their life, but they become bitter and angry, becoming hardened never knowing the joy of their inner beauty much less the inner beauty of others. They have closed the door on their own magnificent qualities, never feeling the joy of loving who they are or realizing their own perfection or the perfection of those around them.

Everyone can become a soft person if they want to be. The most difficult part of becoming a soft person is first finding your own inner beauty and joyfully loving yourself.

Next is seeing the inner beauty of all those around you and joyfully loving and sharing your positive energy. When you do, you will radiate softness, drawing other soft people to you.

For the most part hard people will avoid you. The positive energy that surrounds you makes them feel uncomfortable. But there are hard people who will feel the warmth of your positive energy and want more of it. They will have an innate knowing and a strong desire to become soft.

On the occasions when you are around hard people, you will find they have no negative effect on you. This is because you are wonderfully soft, encased in your own armor of love and beauty. You are centered and nothing can take you off center, not even the negative energy of hard people.

I want to be a soft person, and I want to have soft people all around me.

This is where my thoughts took me today.

Christmas Reflections

Christmas Reflections

My view for this brief moment in time...

I love this time of year. It is a time for me to reflect on all my blessings and thank my Heavenly Father and Jesus for all they have done and continue to do for me. I love listening to Christmas songs, especially 'Oh Holy Night' and the 'Little Drummer Boy'; both songs cause my soul to sing with joy. I especially love the giving of gifts to my family and friends. It is a time I can let them know how much they all mean to me. I love sitting back with dimmed lights, the smell of pine, in awe of a beautiful Christmas tree carefully decorated with angels and such. Oh yes... I love the holiday season. It truly is a time to reflect and have appreciation for so much.

Gratitude is but a secret desire of receiving
even more to be grateful for.

What is gratitude? I guess you could say that I'm on an adventurous pursuit, a quest seeking what genuine gratitude is. I believe this to be something of a selfish endeavor. I want to know the inner joy and blessings that are bestowed on those who are truly grateful and appreciative. There are times in my life I think climbing Mount Everest would be easier than being grateful. At different points in my life's journey I have had disappointments, loss of those I love, hardships of various forms, both emotional and physical pain. During such times it was difficult for me to see the wonderful blessings surrounding me.

Our lives are parallel realities; both abundance and lack exist simultaneously in our lives. Each of us makes conscious choices everyday as to which reality we put our focus and energy. Life is like a garden, we can plant beautiful flowers or we can plant weeds. We make the choice as to which garden we will tend.

When I was a little girl every summer we planted a garden, and I remember how we had to tend it often to rid it of newly sprouted weeds before they grew tall and took over, pushing the beautiful flowers out. It was much easier to get rid of the weeds when they were small and few rather than wait until they multiplied, standing tall and strong. With the weeds thinned out the flowers grew tall and beautiful, becoming strong and dominant pushing out the weeds.

I think our lives are like that. We must focus on the beauty in our lives allowing all that we love to grow and expand, pushing aside the things that make us unhappy. When we choose not to focus on what is missing from our lives but are grateful for the abundance that's present... love, health, family, friends, work, the joys of nature and personal pursuits that bring us pleasure, the darkness fades away and we actually can experience Heaven here on earth.

"There is a calmness to a life lived in gratitude; a quiet joy. "
Author: Ralph H. Blum

We are fortunate to have so much educational material around us to teach us how to have a more happy and joyous life. During the past few years I have read just about every book that has come off the press on the subject, how to find happiness, joy and inner peace. Instructions on creating the lives that we want and to have all that we want. Much of this material has been very helpful to me, but nothing will really work unless you earnestly apply it. I know it is ultimately up to me alone to find my inner joy and happiness. I must go deep within and come to grips with my soul purpose and follow that path. This is a journey that I must take alone, an adventure that is exclusively mine, each step taking me closer to knowing myself, loving myself, appreciating myself and ultimately finding that elusive joy from within.

When I can love and appreciate myself completely and unconditionally, it is then I will fully understand the joy of gratitude and appreciate my life to the fullest. When I finally arrive to this joyful state, I will be able to truly love and appreciate all those around me as well. Each small step of gratitude I take brings me closer and closer to my destination, that of joy.

I am grateful for my life, for each breath that I take. I am grateful for my good health, for my heart and soul and for being able to love and to feel. I am grateful for my precious family; they mean everything to me. I am grateful for my pets and the companionship they provide. I am grateful for my job and my co-workers. I am grateful for all the things I get to do and enjoy. I am grateful for all the places I have been and the opportunities I have had in my life. And there is so much more but I will choose a final one. I am grateful for my Heavenly Father, Jesus and all the angels who love and protect me. I am grateful for the peace and calmness they bring to my life.

May you find inner joy, peace and calmness in your life. And may you always have gratitude, and may you always have enough, making enough into even more.

Love and Blessings...

This is where my thoughts took me today.

Yesterday

Yesterday

My view for this brief moment in time...

As I grow older there is much to look back on in my life. Some days I look back in amazement and joy. But, on the cloudy days I look back in doubt or regret, questioning the choices I made. I wish I had accomplished more and had been more understanding and loving. Perhaps I should have been more selfish to my own dreams and desires. But then I turn right around and wonder if I should have been less selfish and more giving.

There have been times when I could kick myself for not taking advantage of past opportunities that were mine for the taking. Some at the time, I did not realize were as important as they were, and others I just foolishly shrugged away. And then there were the opportunities in my ignorance, I didn't even know existed.

There is so much I could have been, if I had planned my life out just right. Perhaps I could have been a great writer, a doctor or even a lawyer with a Harvard degree. I ponder if any one of those accomplishments would have made a difference in how I feel today. As I look around comparing myself to those who I see as more accomplished than me, the dark shadow of failure starts to grab hold.

I begin to question the decisions of yesterday, wondering what my life would be like if I had made different choices. The list is long of all the things I wish I had done. And today, there is another list of all the dreams of the present. Many times I have felt discourage, wondering if I have ran out of time. Then I question, if all my dreams of the past and the new ones of today were accomplished, would it make a difference in how I feel, anyway? There would surely be something else I would look back on, in either joy or regret, wondering what would be different if I had done it another way.

I have often heard that we are exactly where were meant to be. Keeping that in mind, perhaps there was nothing I could have done, or should have done, to change where I am today. Everything I have done and everything I have gone through has put me exactly where I was meant to be. It seems that every joy and every struggle has had some purpose in my life, and helped me to grow. So, if I look at it from that point of view, there is nothing for me to regret, good or bad that happened yesterday. It may have been terrible at the time, but perhaps it was those really terrible times that gave me the biggest spurts of growth, making me a better person.

I can look back and reflect on how much I've changed because of my experiences, and how much I've learned, from both the joy and the sorrow. Instead of looking at what I didn't achieve or what I could have been, I will look at everything I have accomplished and the wonderful person I am today and be grateful. It is easy to look back and see how perfectly things could have been, but in reality there was no guarantee that it would have worked out the way I imagine. So many things could have gone wrong no matter what decisions I would have made. True, there is the possibility that my life could have been better and I could have accomplished more. But, would it have been better? Surely it would have been different. But, maybe not better.

Our lives are short and it is a pity to waste even a moment in regret. There is nothing positive about regret; nothing good can come from it. I look back at all the wonderful things in my life and feel joy, but for anything that brought me hurt or sorrow, I will consider it an experience that brought me to a better place, where I am now.

I am where I was meant to be, and I am extremely grateful for everything in my life. I look for the joy in all that I am, and all that I have.

With love and blessings…

This is where my thoughts took me today.

A Purrfect Angel

A Purrfect Angel

Dedicated to Ms. Purrfect Purr

07-05-1995 – 01-31-2009

Truth of it is; she was just an ordinary cat.

A kitten abandoned but fortunate to find shelter.

Scared in new surroundings; unsure was her future.

A kitten was my desire, a loving home I could offer.

So many to choose from; more than ten; I saw just one.

She sat amongst the others, but yet she sat alone.

There sitting in the corner was the cutest little tabby of them all.

Independent was her nature, pleasing was not her intent.

I held her close to my heart, but no part of this did she want.

It was her claws and teeth that made it perfectly clear.

This kitty I thought no way, another I would seek.

I looked around to no avail; there was no use to even try.

I looked back again, to the one with the claws and teeth.

You see, she was the one who had caught my eye.

Again I held her close, but to my surprise I heard her purr.

There was no doubt she was the one meant to go home with me.

Many years have passed since that very first day, fourteen to be precise.

This kitty with claws and teeth truly has enhanced my life.

I laughed and played with this kitty; that brought me great joy.

She comforted me during times of loneliness and tears.

Now she no longer sits next to me in her favorite spot.

I'm not able to hear her purrs; she no longer greets me at the door.

There are no more persuasive rubs against my leg, begging to be fed.

Her food dish is empty; it's no longer on the floor.

I remember her sitting there, looking at me with her loving eyes.

I wonder if she knew this would be our last day together.

It all happened so very fast, I really was surprised.

I watched her take one last breath, hoping she would breathe one more time.

She laid there next to me still soft and warm, it seemed as though she was just asleep.

I touched her and looked at her for a long time; it was hard to believe she was really gone.

I'm grateful she was wrapped in my love right to the very end.

It would have broken my heart if she had been alone.

I'm really going to miss this kitty with claws and teeth.

Independent was her nature, pleasing was indeed her intent.

You see, she was the one who had caught my eye.

It will never be the same without this tabby kitty, but I must say good-bye.

She's now in heaven looking down at me with her loving eyes.

As she watches over me, she can hear me when I talk to her.

She runs and jumps in the fields of heaven chasing butterflies.

The happiness she brought me, the comfort and the pleasure is unsurpassed.

I miss you Ms. Purrfect Purr.   Good-bye for now.

The Soul of Angel Bear

The Soul of Angel Bear

Visions of eternity, endless in time, abiding dreams of heavenly treasure troves.

Humming birds dart from flower to flower in the serenity of the celestial groves.

The heart of a lion beats within her soul, bestowing her with courage and strength to endure.

Souls merge enhancing her beauty fusing mortal and spiritual love with penetrating allure.

A sapphire butterfly of transparent splendor adorns her head, a delicate crown of precious jewels of the joyful light.

Golden tresses, a river flowing, radiate the colors of a desert sunset just before the onset of night.

A spiritual being of exquisite angelic beauty; exuding the passions of innocent love.

So beautiful she could only be created in the highest golden realms of God's heavens above.

Gazing upward in awe of the heavenly wonders; awaiting her in God's loving arms.

Indigo clouds floating endlessly creating visions of spiritual lands encased in fairy tale charms.

Impressive splendors, images of divine tranquility placing her in a fixating trance.

A lioness ambles through a meadow of crimson flowers, turning her head so slightly, giving the lion a loving glance.

A Magical Land

A Magical Land

I sit quietly in a fairytale meadow filled with beautiful wild flowers of white, yellow and blue, each one sending a message of God's love to everyone, telling of humility; in darkness revealing the heavenly light.

Two magical Unicorns graze peacefully in a lush green pasture, carefully pushing the flowers aside as they partake of their grassy delight.

In the distance, in awe, I see a powerful waterfall cascading down creating a beautiful stream of lavender and gold.

So beautiful it's as though all the treasures of God's heavens are winding gently through this scenic creation, my thoughts are of heaven… for he who thinks most of heaven will do most for the world, at least, that is what I am told.

A castle sits on a hill looking over the entire meadow, a path descends into the pasture of flowers right next to where a mother Unicorn nuzzles her newborn. Oh such beauty I clearly see, but I'm saddened; for not everyone can see what I see.

Those who have no gratitude for all the blessings God has bestowed on them are blinded to what I see in my magical land.

For them to see… all it would take is just one humble prayer or two saying, "Thank you, to Thee."

A man and a small boy stand in mid stream, fishing poles in hand; reminding me that anger or hatred are like a fisherman's hook, you must be cautious to never get caught by it making your heart hard and bitter.

Forgiveness to others and forgiving yourself is your protective wrap; opening your heart to love will make your glorious soul glitter.

Majestic mountains afar, blending with the rest of the scene, lavender with caps of snow on each one, gazing at their beauty I realize happiness at times takes us by surprise.

We can't always seize on to happiness, but happiness seizes on to us at the breaking of each new day as we sit quietly and watch a beautiful sunrise.

Happiness always looks small while you hold it in your hands, but let it go, and you will learn just how big and precious it is, in a moment … you will know in just a blink of an eye.

It is by attempting to reach the tallest peak at a single leap that so much misery is caused in the world. Take just one step at a time, go slow, one step at a time, just give it a try.

Above the mountain high… oh such a gorgeous sky of lavender, gold, pink and blue, pulling me upward into God's loving arms; never pulling me down in envy or shame.

There is always a certain peace in being what one is; in being that completely and never restricting oneself or sinking into despair through the beckoning door of self blame.

As the golden sun sets, the sky seems to twinkle with its embrace of each beautiful star, oh but perhaps they are not stars at all, but rather openings where our loved ones shine down sending us their love.

Alas... the magical Unicorns have bedded in the lush green grass for the night. I, too, need my night's rest, but before I close my eyes; I must first take a moment to thank God for the magical land He created just for me; with just one stroke of His hand; on His easel in the heavens above.

Reflection in the Mirror

Reflection in the Mirror

Sometimes life seems so dark and dreary, if only I could find away to spread God's light.

So many people... their eyes full a doubt and fear.

I ponder thinking; if only I could be a candle shining so bright.

Or perhaps I could be the reflection of a candle's brightness... just like a mirror.

I would reflect the light on despair that rides on the harsh winds of discontent filling the world with tribulation and strife.

Oh... how nice it would be to make a difference, to help make the world a friendlier place.

To help everyone see clearly the miracle of a single flower and to perceive how it could change their life.

I would reflect the beauty of simple pleasures bringing tranquility, placing a contagious smile on everyone's face.

Aw yes, to shine on a mountain towering above; rising up into fluffy white clouds in awe-inspiring splendor.

I would be the light reflecting brightly at the tip of each peak beautiful and serene, illuminating caps of white forming a heavenly crown.

Alas, all would see a message from God reminding them of His presence and to Him their trust they would surrender.

All would feel the power of His awesome strength, far beyond mortal man; the power of God's loving grace looking down.

Each morning of each new dawn, I would magically fill all hearts with the love they seek.

Oh… how wonderful it would be, if only I were a mirror of light for all wonderful thoughts, each one creating a garden in the minds of all, where all thoughts are seeds.

Helping all to seek not happiness in the distance, but be one of wisdom, wise enough to grow it under their feet.

I would reflect the warmth, and light the way, as each travels their path of life, where they will find their harvest is flowers and not weeds.

Oh if only I were a mirror; reflecting a candle so bright, I would surely light the way.

An Angel's Feather

An Angel's Feather

Golden rays of the sun penetrate the earthly realm, providing warmth sent from the heavens above.

Dainty flowers of lavender growing in the wild; expose their faces to the birth of a new season and God's tender love.

Angels gather in the meadow, fanning their wings creating a soft gentle breeze.

Blue Jays sing of love, their beautiful melody sooths all God's creatures living amongst the trees.

An angelic feather floating peacefully to the ground, before touching, it is carefully embraced by the gentle breeze created by the fanning of angel wings.

With care it is carried to a beautiful forest, drifting silently encased in the splendor of God's early spring.

An exquisite maiden of rare beauty, sits alone in a flower garden, a warm breeze brushes the feather against her soft cheek, a kiss from an angel for which she is not aware.

Here she finds solitude from the chaos of her daily routine, a place to be one with God and sit in loving prayer.

Truly a part of heaven to rest and enjoy, just a few feet away there is a path running through the flowers where children run and play.

Little boys and little girls, all of them loved by their Heavenly Father, each one special in their very own way.

A young couple walking hand in hand surrounded by God's beauty, bound together by golden threads of love, surely a relationship that is rare.

Two heavenly souls walking an earthly path, hearts that are pure and loving, they will always be happy in each other's care.

In the meadow the angels are now resting, surrounded by beautiful marigolds, enjoying the wonderful energy of God's love all around.

Their wings are now still… no longer fanning; two little girls sit close by in awe of a beautiful white feather floating peacefully to the ground.

In a nearby lake two swans glide silently across one side to the other, their reflections upon the water glisten in the radiant golden sun.

Fluffy white clouds float through the sky; wonderful energy of God's love transmits to every living thing on earth, sharing the softness of an angelic feather with everyone.

Autumn Splendor

Autumn Splendor

The harsh summer heat has retreated allowing the coolness of autumn to emerge in its entire splendor.

The hillsides are adorned with beautiful fall colors of orange, crimson and gold.

All of nature gives a sigh of relief; it is now time for the trees to shed their leaves and rest for the winter.

Each awesome peak is capped with a crown of beautiful white snow. Oh, such a sight to behold.

Time itself is such a treasure, your time, my time; our time together, creating memories flowing into deeper and more beautiful hues with each passing day.

Such breathtaking grandeur all around; God's hand at work painting a mural of such exquisite magnificence.

Feel the embrace of God's cool breeze against your cheek, the coldness in your hands as a snowman is created; today you can be a little child at play.

Hear the whispering of the aspen blowing in the breeze, a mystical invitation luring you into a tranquil trance.

Lovers together... become one as they ascend the mountain, imprinting in their minds magical memories of God's magnificent creation.

If you sit quietly you can hear the angels singing above from the clear autumn skies, musical sounds of heaven's best.

The doors of paradise open, displaying all God's beauty, looking up... cloud formations create images that are only limited by one's lack of imagination.

Engulfed in the scent of pine all around, looking down at such majestic elegance, there is so much to be thankful for, even in a world where there is so much unrest.

On the highest peak a view all around, so breathtaking there is no doubt it was created by a higher power.

In reflection of what God's universe entails; there is an overwhelming realization each of us surely is a mere speck in the scheme of God's plan.

Nonetheless, to be so small does not diminish our worth in God's eyes; He loves each one of us no less than if we were the tallest tower.

Each one He gave a heart; each one a warm pulse that contains the sun; each one of us a soul full of love; a gift from God; given to every woman and to every man.

Today a Man
Was Changed Forever

Today a Man Was Changed Forever

Today a man was changed forever from a horrifying tragedy.

Can anyone discern his anguish?
Can anyone feel his pain?
Can anyone see his tears?

An exceptional man lost himself this day; he waned with the fading of the sun as it slipped behind a heavy dark cloud.

Oh the gripping pain within his being; unable to find relief from the piercing dagger impaled in his soul.

Looking up; there are thousands of eyes staring at him; he sees the terror in each face amongst the crowd.

In the clutches of horrifying agony; this dark day has etched its deep scars of guilt within his being, how can he ever emerge from this deep black hole?

Today a man was changed forever from a horrifying tragedy.

Can anyone discern his anguish?
Can anyone feel his pain?
Can anyone see his tears?

Weak from the unbearable anguish, salt from his tears a burning flame to his wounds so fresh.

Oh dear God, release this precious man from this chamber of torture where he is being held against his will.

Unable to erase the Hades visions within his mind, an inferno of his burning flesh.

Sea of red no longer blue; harsh winds destroy the shore, he covers his ears in hopes of escaping the sound of someone's penetrating shrill.

Today a man was changed forever from a horrifying tragedy.
Can anyone discern his anguish?
Can anyone feel his pain?
Can anyone see his tears?

It was an accident, no fault of his, there was nothing he could do to prevent this terrible tragedy, sitting down; he hangs his head in sorrow, knowing he is not to blame.

God reached down with His caring arms wrapping him in a golden cloak of divine love, a shield protecting him from the aberration in his mind.

Angels wipe the tears from his cheeks, staying close by his side helping to ease the unmerciful pain.

In a moment; just like that he was changed, a loving man refined in tragedy, finding love and strength in God and from his angels; their comfort he will always find.

Today a man was changed forever from a horrifying tragedy.
Can anyone discern his anguish?
Can anyone feel his pain?
Can anyone see his tears?

Ball of Light

Ball of Light

A beautiful maiden sits on a grassy knoll amongst daisies of yellow and white, for some time now she has been in deep thought; she ponders what the future will hold for all creatures of God's light.

She does not know what tomorrow will bring, but she has seen the birth of a new dawn and the gracefulness of geese when in flight.

In her hand she holds a ball of light; the brightness pulls her towards the center where perhaps the answers can be found.

The secrets of when the spring will come are not revealed, but she has heard the melody of a robin's song, listening carefully there is no other sound.

She gently reaches down to pick a yellow daisy; brushing it softly across her cheek, she carefully places it in her hair.

The mystery of why God made flowers remains untold, but she has marveled at the beauty of a rose, for nothing else can compare.

The stars in the heavens above twinkle like diamonds radiating in the moonlight; perhaps each one is a heavenly soul waiting for the moment when it is their turn to become a mortal man.

She has held a newborn baby close, but she does not know exactly when and where life began.

Angels come to sit with her as she meditates; the desire to learn the truth is unyielding, she must know all the reasons why.

She has seen a beautiful butterfly in flight, but how can this be... in the beginning it was just a caterpillar and was not able to fly.

She again looks into the ball of light she still holds in her hand, looking deeper and deeper into the center, if only she could see deep enough... just maybe all her questions would be satisfied, but the light is growing dim.

It's not intended for her to know what's waiting just beyond the bend, but she has heard God's word, felt His touch, seen His works, in Him she now believes; the future is in God's hands; so all her trust she faithfully puts in Him.

The Dream Catcher

The Dream Catcher

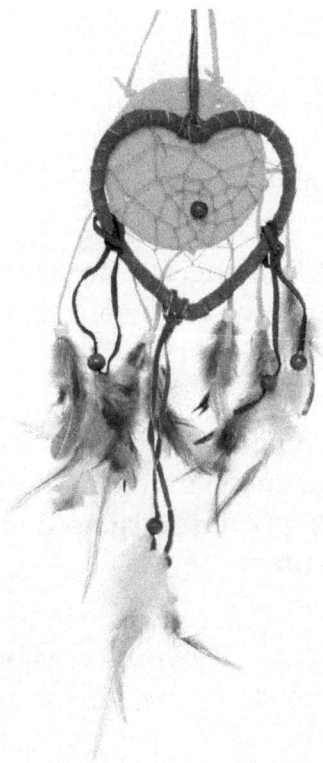

An angelic Indian maiden of exquisite beauty, eyes as dark as the depths of the ocean, long silky hair the color of onyx... sits in a meadow of beautiful lavender flowers, the healing colors of God's heavenly hue.

She silently sits in waiting to catch your most precious dreams, tossing aside the nightmares of the devil, insuring only dreams of happiness and love come true.

As the golden sun sets in the sky, hiding just over the horizon out of sight of one's eye; visions of desires and wants begin to form, your heavenly maiden is waiting to catch any dream that may drift by.

Wolves of white with auras of gold gather at the dreams catcher's door, standing firm to their task; not letting one nightmarish thought come to pass, nothing of evil can get beyond their watchful eye.

She knows the desires of your heart and the goodness of your soul; she spins up a vortex of energy helping form your dreams into a reality.

~ 73 ~

With the help of God and your very own prayers, she is able to take all your wonderful desires, hopes and wishes, spinning them into truths of what your life is and what it can be for all eternity.

In the meadow of dreams; there is beauty flowing all around, in the distance; in the stillness of the night; a light flickers silver and gold, the glitter in each twinkle of a star.

Each special dream is wrapped in gold foil; angels place them one by one on the hearth of God's mantel for all the angels to see way afar.

In the awesome quiet of the night, moonbeams gather their special powers from the energy of the moon's golden rays, wolves howl, keeping all evil at bay; prayers disguised as dreams are answered; each one in God's time.

An Indian maiden chants a song of happiness; a joyous occasion of God's plan in action, bringing forth miracles of joy, gifts from God for the highest of good and love so divine.

The heavens open as the energy of yellow and gold pass through the catcher of dreams, through to her heart where only goodness looms.

She sees only the beauty within your soul, knowing your deepest desires and the treasures of your heart, sending to you though her perfect love a magical kiss every time a flower blooms.

She cries when you cry, she weeps when you weep, her soul cries out in pain when your heart aches in sorrow, she hears your prayers and is a messenger of God making sure He hears each and every word you pray.

A beautiful maiden standing guard each night, diligent to her task, watching carefully not one single dream gets away.

At the start of each new day, flowers open their souls to greet the sunrise, birds sing of joy, prayers answered during the night; your joy is their joy, they could never be more thrilled.

An angelic Indian maiden sleeps in a meadow of beautiful flowers, resting until she is summoned again by the setting of the sun, with love for you she will be there to make sure your dreams will find their way to heaven and God's promise to you is fulfilled.

Your Special Angels

Your Special Angels

Did you know you have special angels who love and take care of you?

They are called guardian angels, and when you were born, God assigned them to watch over you in everything you do.

Each morning when you awake, they are with you to help you greet each new wonderful day.

They dance to the music of the heavenly songs as they watch you and your friends at play.

When the sun is shining over the meadow of beautiful flowers, you can feel their wings wrapped around you in their sweet loving embrace.

Sometimes you feel sad, perhaps something did not go your way, or perhaps someone hurt your feeling, or you fell and skinned your knee, it was one of your special angels who wiped the tears from your face.

That little voice you think you hear but there really was no sound, well... I just thought you would like to know, it is your special angels giving you advice.

Still your sweet mind and listen very carefully to what they have to say, the words they have for you to hear are important, and they will always be precise.

When you are confused and not sure of what you should do, take a moment and ask them softly for their help, you see they are always by your side, ready to help you find the sun so bright.

When someone you love or a friend is sick or in need, all you have to do is ask your special angels to take care of them and to please make everything all right.

As you go throughout your day, you can feel them all around; you will feel a marvelous tingle within your soul, if only you will stop long enough to be aware.

They are there with you; to summon them all you have to do is just say a short little prayer.

If you ever get lost and can't find your way, just remember your special angels are always by your side; they are anxious to help you, if only you will put your trust in them.

When you're happy and having fun, they are singing wonderful sounds of happiness, and if again, you will stop to listen, you will hear them laughing, and each one has a grin.

Still Your Mind

Still Your Mind

Still your mind; in nothing be anxious.

The dark cloud of worry reaches down with its deceitful clutches filling all God's children with doubt and fear, subjecting them to its hellish wrath.

Worry is the master of emotional torment, the destroyer of peace and love, leaving destruction in its path.

Worry will blind you to the answer you are seeking, even when it's right before your face.

Worry is a killer, paralyzing the mind, stealing sleep, causing illness; creating cowards of even the best of men, showing mercy to no one, there is no safe place.

Worry is trust in the unpleasant, the assurance that disaster is coming, it is the belief in defeat and despair; and worst of all it, gives Satan control of your mind.

Worry is the polluted stream that surging through your being drowns hope and faith and every form of optimism; in your desperate search for peace, I guarantee peace is not what you will find.

Worry is interest paid on trouble that has never happened.

Stop it! Stop it! Stop it!

Worry cannot live in the secret place of the most high, it cannot breathe in the atmosphere of faith, and it surely cannot survive the power of prayer.

Climb on the wings of faith into the very presence of God, give thanks and praise Him, worry will vanish and faith will explode, and your heart and mind will be ruled by the peace of God, you will dance in delight and find your very own personal flair.

Be like a tree planted by rivers of living water, knowing your leaves will not wither and you will flourish in whatsoever you do.

When you need the strength to free your mind, ask God for help, for demons tremble when you're on your knees; you're anointed with the power of God and nothing can defeat you.

In time of trouble God shall hide you in His pavilion; protecting you, and He will set you upon a solid rock, lifting your head high, for God is with you and you shall not fear, all you have to do is believe.

Be anxious for nothing, casting all your worry aside, putting your trust in God for He knows the prayers of your heart, you're a favored child of God, simply ask and you shall receive.

The lilies of the fields know this and are at peace, the sparrows that fly in the sky know this, and if you have faith you will know this, yes, He will always be there for you too.

God guides the arrow, He guides the sparrow's flight, there is nothing you are in or that you are going to, that God can't handle, so believe and trust in God's love for you.

God will never leave or forsake you, cast all of your burdens upon Him, and He will sustain you, you're a child of God, and worry is beneath your royal dignity.

You're what you choose to think about, control your thoughts and you can control your world, for the thoughts you think will bring you peace or torment and become your reality...

Still your mind; in nothing be anxious...

Not Far At All

Not Far At All

The despair, the sadness I feel, the longing for your love once more.

I have stopped believing; hoping; all my dreams gone; washed away with the tide.

My soul cries out for your love, your embrace, your sweet lips, desires I try to ignore.

Oh the tenderness of your love no more, within the loneliness of my cold bed, each night I long for you and cry.

Without you I have no purpose, no meaning, and no reason to be my best.

My life seems to be an endless road of nothing but unfilled dreams.

I long for your loving touch; the touch of your hand within mine; your loving words warming my heart bringing peace to my sweet soul so I can finally rest.

An endless play of sorrows; a written script of sadness; listen carefully, and you can hear my impassioned screams?

Oh, I'm here... right here... not far; not far at all.

Can you see me? Oh dearest love; please look close so you can see me.

I'm here... right here... not far; not far at all.

I'm the freshness of a beautiful flower; please look close so your love can find me.
Without you my song is only lyrics, sung with empty words.

Singing souls that are barren, for their light is dim and they have no heart.
I see only faceless images, trying desperately to sing the melody of lovebirds.

I try not to look; not to want you; not to be with you; oh how cruel it is for us to be apart.
I keep falling further and further into a bottomless hollow; into a horrid lonely dark place.

With no water to quench my thirst, I crawl across the hot sands of the desert looking for an oasis to relieve me of my sorrows.
An endless ocean of despair, strong currents take me far away from your embrace.

The longing, oh the longing to feel the gentleness of your soft touch upon my face; bringing forth a beautiful rainbow for all my tomorrows.

Oh, I'm here... right here... not far; not far at all.

~ 90 ~

Can you see me? Oh dearest love; please look close so you can
see me.

I'm here… right here… not far; not far at all.

I'm the freshness of a beautiful flower; please look close so your
love can find me.

Rebecca, an Earthly Angel

Rebecca, an Earthly Angel

"My Gift to Becky"

Angels rejoiced and trumpets played on the day of her birth, an exceptional spirit was now earthbound, but still in God's grace.

Great character, integrity, love and beauty will be her traits; good-bye for now, the golden realms of heaven opened their arms for one last embrace.

She came from a celestial kingdom, through the veil of human creation, a gentle swish like the sound of wings, angels singing in grand jubilation.

Crowned with auburn tresses, sprinkled with golden glitter, a long river flowing, the color of the golden rays of sun, reflecting the light of all the heavenly moons.

Deep sea of warm blue eyes opening the windows of her soul; an array of wonder where goodness looms.

Wings of angels assist her, bringing her gently to earth, pushing away fears of mortal man, bringing forth the beauty of a rose and the wonderful fragrance of night jasmine.

Angels sing, as they watch her grow into a lovely young woman of divine love, delicate angelic beauty, so beautiful she could only have been created in the highest golden realms of God's heavens above.

The doors of heaven open wide with glee, descending a beautiful dove, bringing her an exquisite diamond to love and to cherish for all eternity.

Like a pot of gold at the end of a rainbow where dreams are fulfilled, she gives thanks to God each day, for her husband's sweet love, an earthly heaven they will build.

On golden threads of silver light, God sprinkled them with golden angel dust, arriving at their earthly door, gifts from heaven, three beautiful pearls put in their trust.

Their time together is too short, but powerful and strong, creating cherished memories so dear, feeling the warmth of their devotion, souls bonded for eternity, she knows they will always be near.

Gazing upward in awe of the heavenly wonders, knowing her destiny is in another place, with the escort of angels, fluffy white clouds come to carry her back through the veil, to the awaiting loving arms of God, her soul shining brightly in His grace.

The angels rejoiced and trumpets played on the day of her passing, a gallant spirit now celestial bound, golden wings she is awarded, from the balconies of heaven angels sing.

A young wife and mother who loved with all her heart and soul, a divine sprit who cannot be replaced, good-bye for now, until again you will be in our embrace.

Like the soothing calm of an ocean breeze after the harsh winds are laid to rest, her memory a safe harbor to dock your vessel, storing your love for her in your treasure chest.

Cloud Man

Cloud Man

In Memory of Dr. John A. Day
5-24-1913 – 6-21-2008

In his later years he has come to appreciate the difference between looking and seeing, a powerful awareness of God's beauty nourishes his soul.

This could be any subject matter, but in his case it pertains to the angelic beauty of God's gift of beautiful fluffy clouds, observed daily as he takes his morning stroll.

Looking to the heavens in peaceful meditation, warmed by God's golden touch, looking up towards the heavens, he wears a look of wonder upon his face.

His guardian angel rests upon a cloud watching him create a fairyland of charms, each cloud tells a wondrous tale, in his mind he has disappeared to a special place.

His overwhelming desire pushes him to observe each unique cloud, such a wondrous sight, he watches in awe as each one transforms from moment to moment up in the sky.

Now he is really seeing and not just looking, more than just a visual background to the eye, for him to look to the clouds above there are many reasons why.

You see, clouds and cloudscapes are the greatest free show on earth, costing not a penny to look up at, delighting in such a beautiful visual feast.

Clouds are never exactly the same, each an analogy of a beautiful symphony, a variation of all the golden stars in God's heavenly realm, fluffy white clouds to the west and fluffy white clouds to the east.

The wondrous skies, behold such lucid beauty, combinations awaken the imagination of his inner soul, and colors of the rainbow after a summer rain, oh, so pleasing to his eye in every way.

The sun stretching its golden rays carefully peeks above the horizon, making sure all the golden moonbeams are securely tucked in bed before casting upon the clouds beautiful colors of golden orange bringing the dawn of a new day.

The wind gently blows a feather across a meadow of lovely sapphire flowers, the sun set brings a golden cast of exquisite beauty upon the clouds; a heavenly painting created by God's angels from above.

His earthly soul reaches out to the innocence of nature, gently resting next to a flowing river, along in a beautiful grove of splendor feeling the radiant energy of God's love.

Fluffy gray clouds full of moisture, celestial angels open the gates of a heavenly river, each drop bringing nourishment to earth, and the life force for all living things.

In the skies a beautiful rainbow, mountains and valleys bloom with God's treasures, gifts of love adding beauty to his life, touching him with golden dust from angel wings.

The clouds bring out the child in him, images of elephants, tigers, airplanes and boats; visions of fantasy create laughter and peace within his precious soul, awakening his unfolding hopes.

He gazes up to lands of awesome splendor, magical clouds of wonder, and visions of divine tranquility with the nourishing colors of a kaleidoscope.

www.cloudman.com

Wings of Serenity

Wings of Serenity

Under the cathedral of God's awesome universe a beautiful maiden sleeps peacefully on a soft bed of grass encased by brightly colored flowers, her unconscious mind in the midst of a wonderful dream.

A dream directed by her guardian angels, her teachers from the celestial realms; lessons of wisdom is their gift to this most precious soul which God has put in their loving care.

From God's heavenly scrolls, as she sleeps they teach her the secrets of serenity… guidelines in how to live a mortal life, instructing her how to be happy and have high self-esteem.

As she sleeps, one by one, each pearl of wisdom is transported from heaven down a golden path to where she lies; unaware God is answering her prayer.

Drawn unto her the heavenly light, while her body sleeps, her angels let nothing, but positive energy flow into her life stream.

It is just so easy, so simple you see… her angels orchestrate, all she has to do is dream.

First, live each day fully, without worrying about your problems, try it for at least one day.

Think beautiful, warm, loving thoughts about yourself and others, making up your mind to choose only love and happiness.

Take care of your physical appearance, eat right, get plenty of sleep and exercise, too, always taking time to run and play.

Try not to be better than anyone else, simply be the best you can be, always being kind, thoughtful and loving to others, never trying to impress.

Be aware of your strengths and weaknesses and set your goals to match, decide your values and beliefs, and think about how you would like your life to be.

Review your past, and forgive those who have hurt you; and forgive yourself for those whom you have hurt.

Think about your life experience, lessons learned from the past, let go of guilt and shame for they have little value on your new path, keep looking forward as far as you can see.

Plan what you need to do, putting your most important activities at the top of the list, follow your plan carefully, do not feel afraid, and to the past you must never revert.

Let others know you are there to give, to receive, and to share.

Practice being pleasant and enjoying others, even if it is difficult at first, enjoy the positive energy they have to give.

Keep telling yourself that changing yourself is up to you, you can do anything you put your mind to do, you can succeed, it really is up to you and you can even add your own personal flair.

Remember you do not always need to please others, never forgetting your happiness is your own responsibility, it's your life to live.

As the dawn is drawing near, she begins to stir, not yet knowing what has taken place, unknowingly each pearl from the heavens has been recorded in her subconscious memory.

In this garden of beautiful, colorful flowers, she awakens in the morn feeling forever free from human discord, feeling a magnificent tingle within her soul, feelings of love, harmony and serenity.

Persistence

Persistence

Never give up. Never give up.

It is always too soon to quit, the winner is the one who endures to the end; someone who is too tough to quit; you see, people do not succeed simply by luck or even a destiny that is theirs by God's heavenly design.

Success is bestowed on those who have faith in God and in themselves, succeeding because they are determined to finish the job; plodding on like an Ox... transforming dirt into a beautiful garden... on and on... holding fast to a dream and never resigning.

God hears your prayers, knowing at times your burdens are heavy and hard to bear; He knows that you see before you huge mountains blocking your way.

He knows you're tired and retreat seems like the only logical choice, but each time you kneel down in prayer He lovingly reminds you persistence will make you the winner at the end of the day.

Persistence is not manipulated by lies and deception, it doesn't play the blame game; and surely it never looks back seeing only excuses, deceiving your mind; portraying your future as simply a rerun.

Without persistence disappointments of yesterday bring forth the shadow of doubt, today the fading of hope, and tomorrow the dark deep hole of despair, destroying a colorful rainbow of wonderment yet to come; in reality your life has just begun.

Success cannot be instantly obtained, it is an awesome journey; a wondrous lifelong adventure where patience is truly a virtue and persistence is the key.

God will put you in the fire until you learn that instant gratification is not of heaven's devise; hard work and perseverance is the way, hard work is a reminder nothing is for free.

Persistence is a divine burning within your soul that will carry you through life's ups and downs, even through ridicule and rejection.

Persistence is the strength to keep getting up again and again, pushing obstacles out of your way... nothing is impossible for those who believe, press on, endure, and listen to the angels sing in grand elation.

Giving up is not an option, so walk through the fire of God, it will not burn you, your struggle is proof you have not given up, it is the proof you cannot be conquered.

Persevere knowing nothing is impossible, without persistence your dreams are an illusion, fight back... put on the whole armor of God, look at yourself in the mirror and say, Here is the winner, knowing God always keeps His word.

You're a child of God, special and unique, walking just below the angels... walk like it, talk like it, live like it, yes you can do the impossible; you have the heart of a lion and are strong and bold.

You will be made a pillar in the throne of God, for God loves a winner... you must have persistence to win, so meet the challenge, soar with the eagles, arise on the wings of faith and sit in the presence of God for all to behold.

Never give up. Never give up.

It's always too soon to quit.

Never Before

Never Before

I think you should know she has never loved this way before, tilting his head in questionable doubt, she must tell him more.

Many years gone by, other loves in her past, what makes this love so different from the ones that did not last?

Never before has her feeling soared so high, with every thought of this magnificent man.

Never before was there a man, who truly deserved so much love and praise, she is his best fan.

The list of reasons is a mile long, so many that needs mentioned, but on her list respect and trust are at the very top.

Kindness and unselfishness emanate from his soul like the moisture in a raindrop.

Dependable, a man of his word, someone she knows can be counted on, always there for her and not ever aloof.

Never before has she known a man with such integrity, he would never intentionally hurt her, always telling her the truth.

Through her poems she sings her melody of happiness, an opera of songs illuminate from her soul and her heart.

Beautiful sapphire blossoms, hundreds from each star, float to earth, landing gently on her flower cart.

Never before has she been treated so lovingly, his thoughts and actions are always encouraging, accepting of who she is, not thinking twice of mistakes of the past.

There is never one harsh word or criticism of any kind; blue skies of sunshine radiating from his soul, the days are never overcast.

He treats her with respect, never trying to rewrite the blue print of who she really is, her dreams riding on fluffy clouds; he never tries to shatter.

Listening to her every word, he lets her know how much he cares, making sure there is nothing the matter.

They cherish their time together, their love for each other is precious and dear, without each other the flowers would weep.

Nights together astir, contentment and peace, nights filled with love and the sound of his voice just before going to sleep.

My Angels
Are Always Near

My Angels Are Always Near

When I have no one to turn to and I am feeling kind of low.

And when there is no one to talk to and there is no where I want to go.

I search deep within myself to find the love inside my heart.

A feeling that lets me know my angels are there, they have always been with me from the very start.

A smile then appears upon my face and the sun begins to shine.

I hear a voice, soft and sweet, saying, everything will be just fine.

At times it may seem that I'm alone, but I'm never really by myself at all.

I always have my angels near and if I ever need their help; all I have to do is just give them a call.

An angel's love is always there, on that you can depend.

They will always stand behind you and will always be your friend.

Through darkest hours and brightest days, my angels see me through.

No matter how busy they seem to be, no matter what, they have always been there for me.

And I know that if you call on your angels, they will be there for you too.

Lovers Tears

Lovers Tears

He sees her beauty and the sweetness within, oh such agony reaching deep in his soul, if only he could mend her broken heart.

She looks into his eyes; the window of his soul; revealing to her all the goodness within, the reasons she was drawn to him right from the start.

He holds her close to him in his loving arms, feeling her warmth and the gentleness of her unending love.

She feels the beating of his heart, his tender touch, his love was created in the heavens above.

He kissed her sweet lips, his love over whelming, a life of its own, but yet he turns the other way, trying to outrun his fear.

She touches his soft silky hair, golden love radiating from her soul, her inner demons are pushing him away, further and further away; a treasure so dear.

He looks into her caring eyes, gently wiping a tear from her cheek.

She trembles in fear, unable to hold back her tears; finding it difficult to speak.

Torments of the past are in the way, such relentless agony from which there is no escape, unable to find solitude, for him there is no place to rest.

Her issues unresolved, painful rejections in her past create illusions of dark evil torments of deceit, waging war against her; this battle will be her test.

He is alone, fighting his personal war against the hurtful betrayals of the past, a war that must be fought in the solitude of his soul, a time when they must be apart.

Alone, she battles the evil soldiers of Satan, clever in their deception of reality; visions of pain, loneliness and rejection, this fight must be won before their lives together can again start.

He fought long and hard with angels by his side; love, faith and prayer were his weapons, to him the spoils of victory ... his life with her has just begun.

She fought relentlessly, determined their love would not wither, trust in God is her weapon, angels fight along her side, a victorious war, souls joined together as one.

Fly My Love

Fly My Love

I held you tight with every fiber of my being; to love you forever was my aim.

So terrified if I closed my eyes for even a second you would surely disappear.

To put you in a cage or lure you into a trap; please believe was never my intent.

A precious man of such unique perfection, all I ever wanted was your love so dear, forever near.

Unaware that you could hardly breathe, I kept you ever so tightly in my suffocating grip.

You tried to tell me, you tried to make me understand; but I did not listen; your warnings I did not hear.

More nights and days you would stay away; the tighter my grasp, away from me I did not want you to slip.

Not wanting to lose this precious man I loved so much; I held on ever so tight because of my unrelenting fear.

Fly my love, fly away and discover who you really are.

Fly... fly with the wind; soar with the angels; find your way; enjoy every moment of your flight.

Fly high above the mountain tops into the heavenly skies; see the glitter of every star.

Fly high, my love, until you can see the rainbow within your soul, oh such a glorious sight.

The cage door is open; the time is now for you to spread your beautiful golden wings.

Wondrous is the awesome blue sky, a playground of magical dreams waiting to come true.

You have things to do, you have much to learn about yourself; you're not attached to any strings.

Find your truth, live your truth and become your truth; realize your radiant hue.

Discover the golden essence of who you really are; a man of compassion and love for all mankind.

The sky goes on for all eternity; soar to the highest of heights until you find what you are looking for.

Waiting for you at the end of your journey is a beautiful white dove carrying a message of love from an angel; perhaps you will return if love in another you do not find.

A day or perhaps two, I will wait just beyond the bend; but no matter the road you choose, may love always be with you forever more.

Fly my love, fly away and discover who you really are.

Fly… fly with the wind; soar with the angels; find your way; enjoy every moment of your flight.

Fly high above the mountain tops into the heavenly skies; see the glitter of every star.

Fly high, my love, until you can see the rainbow within your soul, oh such a glorious sight.

Fly my love, fly away and discover who you really are.

Five Little Fairies

Five Little Fairies

Someone once told her that fairies have magical powers and can make all dreams come true.

So, the other day she went to the store and bought five beautiful fairies made of porcelain and gold, more than one would make the odds better, this she knew.

Each one uniquely painted all the colors of the heavens, adorned with fragile wings of gold, sprinkled with precious silver moon dust.

She gave each one a loving name, carefully choosing a special place for each, she placed them throughout the house, her prayers she has put in their trust.

Each day at the break of dawn, the suns golden rays reach down from God's heavenly realms touching each fairy with the powers of the celestial light.

Empowered with God's will; each fairy given a detailed plan, in just a blink of an eye, just like that a dream becomes a reality… in God's grace this is done; to each fairy it is such a delight.

Filling each room with God's sweetness and love, spooling up all the pearls of each and every dream, taking them to a heavenly meadow where they can grow.

There they are nurtured by all of God's heavenly hosts, blessing them with deeds and thoughts of purity and truth, in them the rivers of dreams fulfilled will flow.

There is much to do before the harvesting of a dream, she must make herself worthy, working hard at becoming the best she can be, there is no time to delay

No longer afraid of the future, understanding what it means to really love, thanking God for His blessing, she kneeled down to pray.

A future full of golden sunshine, for her there will be only joys and no more sorrows.

Each morning there will be only beautiful golden sunrises; there will only be wonderful tomorrows.

To this day the fairies continue to fill each room with the blessings of God's pearls from the heavens above.

As instructed by God, they stay close keeping a careful watch with all their heavenly love.

Everything Is a Miracle

Everything is a Miracle

If only you could see the miracle of a single flower, looking close at the clarity of its intricate pattern, surely your whole life would change.

A beautiful cloud in the sky, forever changing in design, it's a child's wonderland of fantasy, a collage of images constantly being rearranged.

The wind blowing gently across a field of corn, a farmer now resting, his seeds are sown and at the present his work is done, his prayers are said; now he and God wait patiently for the seeds to grow.

Putting your faith in God's hands is not always simple; sitting back relaxing your mind is not easy to do, with the help of angels your faith can be strong making your beautiful soul glow.

Take the time to enjoy each day, feel within your soul the beauty all around, never living your life as though you had lots of days ahead, for you, there may be no tomorrow.

Always remember, whatsoever is within you that feels, thinks and desires, is something celestial, divine, and consequently imperishable, constantly let yourself feel the warmth of God's eternal love, even in times of sorrow.

Adversity knocks at the door never knowing who it's looking for, reach out your hand, introduce yourself to your inner soul, your true charter is unfolding towards God's heavenly light, perhaps though you will buckle in the darkness of the hellish realm when faced with the burden of unwanted stress?

Look at everything as though you were seeing it either for the first or the last time, living everyday to the fullest, living in the Glory of God, never wanting more and needing less.

Security is an illusion, not even in nature does it exist, be not fearful as you live your life, the evil torment of fear reaching out it's evil curse takes away all that can be, making it less, life is a daring adventure or nothing at all.

There is no one luckier than he who thinks himself so, for he who can find contentment with little will be blessed, but those who are not content with much have met the impossible and have further to fall.

May the road of life greet you with a smile, may the wind always be at your back, may the rain fall soft upon your fields, may you always feel loved, and may God hold you lovingly in the palm of His hand.

You're braver than you know, stronger than you seem, much smarter than you think, and most importantly, you're one of God's precious children loved unconditionally no matter where you stand.

The passages of life are not always smooth, the seas can be rough, the darkness of the night never ending, persistent strength is needed to weather the dooming storm, the spoils of the victor will be the joy of sunshine, you have no choice but to win.

The skies are gray and dreary, rivers of tears pour from above, and relentless fears of loneliness rip at your soul, angels sent to remind you that you must first endure the rain in order to see a beautiful rainbow in the sky again.

Butterfly of Love

Butterfly of Love

A beautiful butterfly, a butterfly of love, no longer burdened, now able to soar above.

Showing you how to release the tears, hurts and anger of the past, to know you have love and friendships that will forever last.

Encouraging you to not lose sight of all God's wonderful untold gifts and blessings that have been sent to you on angel's wings, teaching you to love yourself, realizing what a unique and wonderful person you are, created in God's beautiful season of spring.

Giving you the faith to preserve a trusting attitude toward life, realizing there will always be trials, tribulations and undeserved strife.

Helping you to know only triumph will prevail; you have played your role well for you have passed the test, and showing tremendous strength and character to all, knowing you have done your very best.

The past is old and gone; your destiny is in another place, and your future is new, shining brightly before you in God's grace.

Your story is not over; your work is incomplete, a new path awaits; you now have new challenges and adventures to greet.

For all those around you, friend and foe, you're true character they all know, your head remains high, even though you were wronged, you will arrive powerful and strong.

Your friends and family are with you, cleaving to you in all you do, you're blessed with God's love and you're loved and protected by your angels too.

Accept all the love around you and open your heart, you're beginning a brand new wonderful life, like the butterfly, you have a new start.

Assume the Very Best

Assume the Very Best

Your thoughts are strong and powerful, each one you must safely guard, make sure what you think is what you want your life to be.

If you can keep your thoughts on a positive note, always assuming the very best; then you will be creating a much happier life for you and for me.

It is sort of like going to the grocery store to buy all the things you like and want; each item that you want; you carefully place in your shopping cart.

To go down the aisles looking at everything you don't want, but still buying it and taking it home, I am sure you will agree would not be very smart.

So, when you think a thought you do not like or want, it is the same as bringing it home to be part of your daily life.

If you have a choice to choose the things you want most or the things you do not want, I think it would be much wiser to choose the things that would bring less strife.

Think of all the wonderful things you want in your life, visualize yourself doing them and enjoying the feelings that they bring throughout each and every day.

Dwell on the goodness all around you and never on the things that bring you unhappiness or diminish your life in any way.

Only think about how smart you are and all the things you like to do and want to achieve, never for one second thinking that you can't, always keeping your goals in sight.

Always give those around you the benefit of the doubt; assuming the very best of them and you will be surprised at how they will usually prove you right.

I cannot stress the importance of never thinking thoughts you do not want, for if you do I assure you most of the time these thoughts will undoubtedly come to pass.

Think about all the adventures you would like to have, or perhaps even a college degree, if you focus on these wonderful thoughts you will surely be at the head of your class.

Look in the mirror, taking the time to really look at yourself, looking deep within your soul seeing your beauty and the wonderful person you really are.

Never ever put yourself down in any way, this I cannot stress enough... for what you think or say, I assure you that is what you will be, so make all your thoughts happy and positive, because then you will be a shining star.

Be thoughtful and kind, generous and loving to everyone you know, never thinking ill of them and hoping their lives will be happy and right.

By doing this, you will bring wonderful things into your life; you will have happiness untold and you will be a bright shining light.

A New Mother

A New Mother

"Dedicated to Carson and Ollie"

One beautiful evening she looked up to the heavens asking God if He would send her a baby boy, wanting so much to have a child of her very own.

The words of her prayer were heard by all the heavenly angels, each one relaying her heartfelt request to God in the realms of heaven where every star is a beautiful rhinestone.

She was a gallant sprit, one of God's most precious souls, both in heaven and now on earth, her request He could never deny.

Without a moment of hesitation or any delay, a message brought by an angel… to her, He sent His reply.

Her prayers answered; a golden scroll of God's loving words; telling her the summer would bring her a very precious angel from the heavens above.

You could hear the heavenly harps as angels sing songs of joy, for a very tiny little angel would soon be bound for earth and would be surrounded with a new mother's love.

She was overjoyed with God's exceptional news; the first thing she did was give thanks to the heavens for such a wonderful blessing, asking God to please watch over this child in design, making sure he arrived safely and sound.

As the months went by this mother in waiting became even more beautiful, her soul glowed; radiating love from within, the sweetness of bright flowers in her heart could surely be found.

It was a beautiful morning in July, the angels rejoiced and trumpets played on this day of his birth, a bright spirit was now earth bound, but will always remain in God's grace.

One by one each angel said good-bye, knowing one day he would return, in answer to a prayer, he went to his new mother's embrace.

Happiness so pure and right; all the heavenly stars twinkle at each beat of this new mother's heart, love unsurpassed, a mother looking at her beautiful child for the very first time, a miracle of God, which no one can deny.

Two beautiful souls inside and out, a mother and a son; each unique; but still so much alike, both have earthly wings and are not afraid to fly.

Enjoying life together loved and cherished, fun and adventurous; each living life to its fullest, making each day a delight.

Sweet and loving with hearts of gold, grateful for each other, two beautiful souls making all those around them happy and bright.

A Beautiful Flower Smiles

A Beautiful Flower Smiles

The sun stretching its golden rays carefully peeks above the horizon, making sure all the golden moonbeams are securely tucked in bed, each and every one.

The rising of the sun brings the beauty of a fresh dawn, an extraordinary day; the day God's golden rays touched two souls planting the seeds for a new love to spawn.

The wind gently blows a feather floating free within its breeze carrying an elegant sapphire flower so tender, laced with diamonds, gently placing her next to a flowing river, alone in a beautiful grove of splendor.

Across the knoll over the horizon, lies a meadow full of lovely, golden daffodils, among them one is different, standing very tall; God's most cherished of them all.

A radiant golden flower, the color of the sun encased in a ruffled frame, reaching towards the heavens, loved by all in the meadow, bunched in the middle of a few, this his home he will proclaim and finding a love to share it with is his aim.

Even though he was not alone, desire for a love kindled deep within his soul; reaching out over the horizon he finds a flower alone in the grove; an angel resting peacefully amongst the lush green grass, his soul meshed with hers, feeling the burning flame of love from within.

Touching her with a gentle tap, his loving emerald eyes betraying what is truly in his heart, his soul reaches out to hers, joining together as one, wrapped in the warmth of each other, their love perfect from the very start.

Knowing the warmth of her sweet nectar, he stays with her through the night, their love for each other growing, her fears of the darkness diminished, for both being together feels so right.

Two, heavenly treasures bounded for eternity, loving him with all her heart, a beautiful angel no longer alone in her grove, sharing her life with him is such a delight, she kneels down in prayer asking God to bless them making sure they never part.

Grateful for his love, angels sing with her, God's blessings descend from the heavens above, hearts never broken, blessed by the heavens they will always be together, only words of love are spoken.

In the distance the wind gently blows another feather floating free within its breeze, picking up an elegant sapphire flower so tender, laced with diamonds, gently placing her next to a flowing river, alone in a beautiful grove of splendor.

A Grandfather's Love

A Grandfather's Love

She had the most beautiful wings of white with a slight bluish tint, her halo shined of gold with bits of silver moon dust that made it glitter, before leaving she put them in safe keeping in God's heavenly drawer.

He remembers the day the heavens opened and sent him a beautiful granddaughter, an angel so precious all the other angels wept with tears of joy when she passed through the earthly door.

Such a beautiful baby, a treasure to behold, so tiny and precious, a little angel sent from the heavens above.

He watched her through the nursery window as she soundly slept; observing her tiny little fingers and tiny little feet, his soul was touched, this little girl is very special; she will be easy to love.

As he held her for the first time, the heavens opened wide, he could hear the angels sing of her beauty and the sweetness of her soul.

A granddaughter so precious, bringing joy to his life through each passing year, a soft and gentle little girl, but don't let her size fool you, she can be a real handful.

Sometimes she can wrap him around her little finger; you see there is no way he could refuse this irresistible little girl's request.

He remembers the day she came to help him at the shop, they talked for an hour about all kinds of stuff, enjoying the break from his work, he thought her company was the best.

A camping trip to Black River, a memory he will never forget, "When will we be there?" she continually asked. "In just fifteen minutes," he replied, she was unaware his answer was just in jest.

Yes, his special little angel is growing up so very fast, today is her birthday, a beautiful young lady, confident and smart, she is his precious heavenly light.

She grows more and more beautiful with each passing day, a pleasure to be with all of the time, a treasure sent from heaven; to him she is a wonderful delight.

Colors of the Rainbow

Colors of the Rainbow

The heavenly rains bathe all God's creations, bringing a beautiful blue sky of brilliant sunshine, fluffy clouds of silver and white, a miracle overhead, a rainbow sent from heaven reminding us of God's love, she watched in awe at such a exquisite site.

Looking up at the heavens, the colors of the rainbow remind her of the man she loves.

The vibrant colors of the spectrum, each one representing qualities of his soul, her love for him never wavers; the angels play a melody on their harps, telling of her love with each strum.

Violet signifies the dignity of his being, a favored angel in the heavenly realm, one of royalty, an angel of great wealth and unlimited power, protecting all of God's golden words written on scrolls stored on a mountain top in a heavenly tower.

Indigo the energy of his soul, an inner voice guiding him through life with certainty and creativity, a consciousness to his spiritual path of clarity, faith, bringing forth truth in all things, harmony of mind, protecting all that is good with integrity.

Emerald eyes; the color of the ocean, bringing forth harmony and balance, reaching deep within the window of his soul, where lies joy, tranquility, love and devotion.

Golden like the independent sun, generating power sustaining all of life, rising every morning with grand luster, the gaiety in his heart shines down with such perfection, strengthening all he touches with a gentle warming, diminishing all dissension.

Pink the color of his gentle loving soul, the beauty of all God's flowers are within his being, looking down from heaven the angels watch over him in the meadow below.

Red of passion and vitality, forceful and strong like the wind pushing a sailboat safely to shore, living his life adhering to his convictions, loyal and true to all, his generosity unlimited giving all he has and more.

God Sent Two Angels

God Sent Two Angels Today

God sent her two angels today, a message saying everything was going to be okay.

An important communiqué, his love they wanted to convey.

Their caring sweetness creates a rainbow; such a beautiful array.

They let her know the skies are a brilliant blue and never have been gray.

He sees the silver and gold of her beautiful love, a love he would never betray.

The sadness of her soul, torments of her heart, to him they will relay.

His decision influenced by the fears and hurts of the past, she must understand this is the reason for the delay.

His love an endless river flowing towards the treasures of her heart.

Her soul the gateway and in her love he will find the way and by her side the angels stay.

They sing beautiful melodies of happiness, and in the meadows they play.

She sent a lovely bouquet of flowers to the angels from above.

She gives a prayer of thanks to her Heavenly Father, for sending His angels with a message of his love.

Love for an Eternity

Love for an Eternity

A young man and a young women sit quietly in peaceful prayer, their love for one other radiating from their most inner souls, a fire within burning to know, kneeling they ask God for His wisdom he might share with them the key.

Oh Dear Lord, loving and kind, please won't you tell us how to keep our love for each other strong. How can we make this earthly love last an eternity?

Each word of their prayer became a musical note radiating in the atmosphere, magnifying into a beautiful song of profound love finding its way through the celestial veil and to the loving heart of their Heavenly Father.

Two of His children kneeling in prayer, reaching down He touches their souls with His loving hand, letting them know He has heard their prayers and has felt their love... their prayers answered, eternal love promised... for all eternity they will be together.

For you to be in love with one another, you must commit yourself freely, always being sincerely interested in each other's well being, happiness and needs.

Pay attention to each other's needs, fulfilling those needs to the best of your ability; always planting positive and loving seeds.

If one feels lonely and has need of the other, the other will be there, if in that loneliness one needs to talk, the other will listen, if one needs to listen, the other will talk, be loving in both words and deed, never forgetting to display your love.

If one needs strength of human touch, the other will touch them, if the other needs to be held, the other will hold them, if one needs fulfillment of the flesh, the other will give that also, but only with love blessed by the heavens above.

You must try to remain constant so you will never be misunderstood, this way you will never be frightened of an occasional mood, gaining strength through each other's stability.

Do not defer or neglect your love for each other, display your love each and every day, for each day is a life time, if you wait until tomorrow it may never come; for that is a reality.

The degree of love you give each other is determined by your understanding and awareness of God, of love, and of truth.

You must give as much love as you can, teaching each other how to give even more, and remember each other you must comfort and soothe.

Give each other unconditional love, never holding love back, this is the answer, love feeds the soul of both man and woman, keeping the flame burning for all eternity.

In the silence, when the other has nothing to say, look into each other's eyes, give a simple touch or hold each other in a loving embrace, or perhaps give a sweet kiss, this says I love you in so many ways without even saying a word.

A young man and a young women rise to their feet, looking to the heavens they thank God for His lessons on love, these pearls of wisdom they will never forget.

Now they have the key, yes indeed, now they have the key to keeping their love alive for all eternity.

The Merging of Two Souls

The Merging of Two Souls

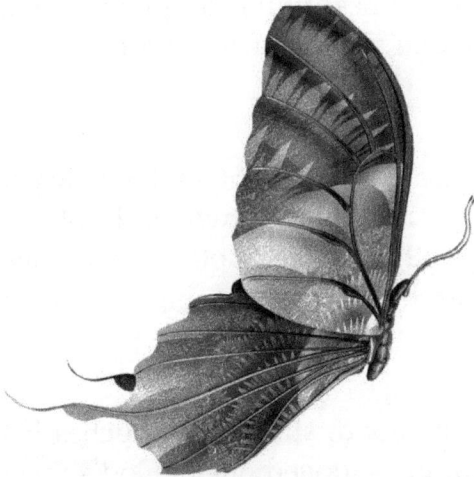

God's radiant light struggles to penetrate the hopelessness of dissipating dreams, the flowers of her soul have withdrawn hiding their faces from the heavenly beams.

Visions of an eternity with the man she loves, fading off into the distance, every fiber of her being is hanging on in resistance.

A treasure, a rare diamond sent to her from God, a precious soul worthy in every way, a misunderstanding, and her feelings hurt, before thinking she sent him away.

Angels stay close by her side encouraging her, helping her make it through the day, wrapping their wings around her, comforting her in love, helping her to have faith God will make everything okay.

In the serenity of the celestial groves flowers weep with sadness, butterflies in their great wisdom flutter from flower to flower spreading good tidings of tomorrow's happiness.

She knows within his soul beats the heart of a lion, the life force of a tiger, bestowing him with the courage and strength needed to face his fears believing their love for each other will endure.

Her visions of eternity, endless in time, happiness and gratification, God's celestial plan, so beautiful it could only have been created in the highest golden realms of heaven by God's loving design.

In the meadow honeybees spread joyful light of their sweet nectar from flower to flower, a merging of two souls of the heavenly universe, meshed together, to each other their love they bestow, vows made to each other in the highest of all places; God's celestial tower.

A beautiful rose, an exquisite diamond, she gently touches his brow; knowing without a doubt he is indeed one of God's most cherished; his heart flutters in ecstasy; he cannot help but respond, the warmth of her soul overflowing with love's fervency creating between them an eternal bond.

Their fears created in the drama of days past are now smothered in certainty and resolute love, they share burning passions of desire, bodies touching in the night, souls meant for each other, chorales of angels sing joyfully in the heavens above.

The flowers of her soul open their faces to the loving rays of the brilliant sunlight; birds sing songs of love, fluffy white clouds float endlessly creating visions of a wondrous future full of love, promises sent from heaven on the golden wings of a dove.

Protect His Precious Soul

Protect His Precious Soul

You must love yourself before you can truly love him, it doesn't matter how much you protest to love him if you don't love yourself; without loving yourself first, you can't really love him.

You must take the time to first become exactly what you want him to be, if this you choose to neglect, I assure you your future with him looks rather dim.

You must face yourself knowing your truth, then strive to be the very best you can be, if these things are ignored, you surely won't find what you're looking for.

But first you must choose a man who values integrity; to you he will always be true, this you must be sure before you even allow him through your door.

The treasures of your soul are precious, cautiously give them away, be wise in your choices, and safeguard your treasures at all cost.

If your welfare is not his main concern, on him your treasures will be lost.

Pay attention to your inner voice; carefully listen to the soft voices of your angels too, knowing they are always near.

Put your mind at rest, enjoy the beauty surrounding you, quiet yourself and listen to God's messages radiating loud and clear.

Kneel down to pray asking God if this relationship He approves and for you is this man right?

If it is meant to be, your heart will surely let you know, your inner soul will beam with love and your entire being will tingle in delight.

At first hold yourself in restraint, be cautious, by all means don't rush, and wait until you are sure before you let him know just how much you care.

In the beginning don't be too quick to reveal too much too fast, you must at first discern what you share.

For a commitment do not push, creating fear you must avoid, be wise; let him go at his own pace.

Let him have the lead, be confident and patient knowing you need not rush, then your relationship will move forward at the pace it should to a wondrous place.

Give him time for his love to grow, be kind and loving, and then a bond between you will be the glue.

Let him march to his own drummer; give him the chance to radiate the beauty of his own precious hue.

Give him space, so he can stay connected to his own divine power, neither of you should ever lose sight of your personal truth just because you have chosen to be together.

Always remember you are two precious loving souls bonded for all eternity, never do anything to him you would not have done to you, what hurts one always hurts the other.

Never take away his freedom to be himself, always allow him to be himself, never trying to change him into someone he's not.

Protect his precious soul; he is a diamond, so polish him with beautiful compliments and appreciation, always thinking good of him with your every thought.

Now if he is wise, he will read this too, and realize all of this pertains to him just as much as you.

Then he will know how to protect your precious soul too.

Unselfish Love

Unselfish Love

The skies are not as blue as they were yesterday; for them the golden sun is not shining quite as bright.

Growing up is not easy, now there is no choice; she must now face the fact that Gods loving angels are always right.

Her love for him is strong and honestly true, but she over looked his needs, focusing only on her own selfish desires.

This was not done intentionally I want you to know, thinking she was doing her best; she had not yet learned what unselfish love requires.

From the heavens her prayers are answered, loving angels surround her with their golden ray of divine love.

Teaching her painful lesson, thoughts and actions that need to be changed, in quiet meditation she is submerged in wisdom, direction given from the heavenly scrolls above.

Her heart yearns for his touch, the sound of his voice with such loving words, difficult lessons to be learned, she prays each day that God will provide her with the strength to endure.

She wonders if he can feel her love and the burden of her remorse; striving to change, no longer will her selfish desires have their magnetic allure.

The angels can see the love in her soul, the pain of her broken heart, caused from her very own hasty mistakes, she asks God to please make things right, for her another chance perhaps he will give.

The angels in their loving compassion let her know how much he longs for her, the trials and tribulations he is facing and of his relentless love, you see without her he does not want to live.

Their separation is a time for their souls to grow together in selfless love, in the care of beautiful angels they are learning just how much they mean to each other.

His thoughts of her are beautiful like the rainbow full of color and brightness; she is the fresh air after a wonderful rain, soft as a cloud, for all of eternity his love for her will go on and on forever.

As she learns these lessons of love, her thoughts are of him, a man worth every second of this painful change, she prays soon they will be together.

Being with him is what is important, but between them from this day on, there must be only unselfish love for one another.

Whispers of Love

Whispers of Love

Listen carefully and you can hear the whispering wind rushing through the aspen trees.

Soft whispers of love echo in the stillness of the night; as she lies in his fiery embrace.

He must master the whispering winds; only then can he harness the intense energy of his love, setting his passions at ease.

A flame burns from within, a raging fire out of control; burning desires causing his heart to race.

Hear the whispers of love within the forest as aspen leaves flutter in the summer breeze.

In the distance just a few feet away, a beautiful blue bird sings of love, attempting to change a fairly tail dream into a reality.

Feeling the intensity of his passion, he looks upon her angelic face as she so soundly sleeps, a precious jewel, this moment he will surely seize.

Her soft hair gently falls across his cheek, as if struck by cupid's arrow; he feels the warmth of their love in its totality.

Oh the wonderment of love dancing in the whispering wind; passion souring to heights of ecstasy; thawing the snow-capped mountaintops.

On the wings of a beautiful white dove their love sours through heavenly cathedrals in the highest of the sky.

Listen closely and you can hear the whispers of their eternal love; listen carefully for it never stops.

Feel the warmth of loves embrace, wondrous is this life they will share; looking upon her sweet face he gave a contented sigh.

Her beauty none surpass, an earthly angel he has found, surely this must be God's heavenly plan.

This night he floats upon a cloud drinking wine with the gods, surrendering willingly to the passions of his soul, for him there is no retreat.

He has risen above the earth; above the clouds and beyond, souls meshed as one, this woman and this man.

Listen closely to the wind blowing in the trees and you can hear the whispers of their love, together their lives are complete.

Whispers of love...   Whispers of love blowing in the wind...

To The Man I Love

To The Man I Love

Ask yourself; are you going to fulfill your destiny?

Oh yes, we know you feel you love her and that you enjoy her company.

But, do really know what you feel deep down within your heart and soul?

Do you have what it takes to really search deep within, to feel feelings you so desperately try to elude?

We seem to know more about how you feel about her than you do; so tragic, but true.

You put up shields to protect you, wanting an affair with her.

Yet it really isn't what you want. Oh yes, wanting more, yet afraid of commitment.

You put up boundaries that hold you prisoner, so afraid to do what you really want to do.

You would like nothing better than to settle down with her in your own loving home.

Together you would live out your lives in comfort and happiness.

What are you afraid of?

Oh dear one, please you must give this a lot of thought.

Are you afraid to spend too much time with her, fearing you will get to close and want to be with her more and more?

You see her as an angel, but you're afraid of being trapped.

Memories of past experiences have become your prison.

Fear finds excuses and other things to do, keeping you from having to make decisions or choices, setting boundaries that only entrap you.

What is the purpose behind your personal beliefs?

Can you let yourself be led where your heart takes you?

If so, then for your future we see a wonderful vision.

Ask yourself; are you going to fulfill your destiny?

Oh yes, it's coming to the time, now!

When you must make a decision pertaining to your future and what your future holds for you.

The time has come; you must be able to choose and not succumb to your age-old fears.

It is time for you to believe in yourself knowing you deserve the very best; you have paid your due.

The time has come, you must let go of the past hurts and go forward to love in your golden years.

For you to be able to lead your own life; a life without fear these are the things you must do.

You must face yourself squarely looking in a mirror, facing yourself in truth.

You must learn to know your truth.

You must learn to live your truth.

You must learn to always be the example of your truth.

You must be able to realize your truth and take courage in stepping forward in that truth.

You must plan for your future and live your life in love, happiness and long-term oneness of mind, knowing and loving the reality of your life!

It is time to take a good look at your life and your relationship.

Yes, you must take a good look at your relationship.

There is an ending, a new beginning is about to unfold.

Realize you must let go of your old thoughts and fears and stop running from yourself.

You must take a good look at yourself and face yourself in truth.

Again we say, face yourself in truth!

Make way for the new cycle of life to take hold.

Clear your mind of all obstacles, some of which you put in your own way through your fears.

You may now realize just how confused you have been in your thinking.

You may think you have lots of time to straighten it all out, but this is not the case.

Search deep within. Discern what is of genuine value and what is not.

You are at the crossroads right now and if you are not careful, you can take a wrong turn and you will never find a happy and fulfilling life for yourself.

Look back in your life, the time is now. Your fears you must face.

How many wrong turns have you taken?

How many times have you made the same mistake over and over again?

On the other hand, take a good look at all the good that now surrounds you.

Rid yourself of all fear! Fear can destroy you, making you choose all kinds of wrong decisions.

There will be a time when you will regret such thoughts and actions.

There will come a time when you may find it too late to make the changes necessary for you to have the love, the peace, the companionship, the happiness, the joy, the fulfillment and a wonderful life for the rest of your life.

When you look ahead constructively, you can plan for abundance and prosperity in your life, enriching your future to be the best for you.

Think carefully, without fear. Be wise in all of your decisions.

Ask yourself are you going to fulfill your destiny?

Do you want her bad enough to put all your fears aside and take a chance?

You have to step out on faith alone!

Believe when you take that leap of faith you will grow wings and you will surely fly.

Feel the fear, but yet believe in yourself.

Believe in her, believe in your angels and believe in God.

Do not live in regret of losing the woman you love, the best thing that has ever happened to you.

Don't let her slip right through your fingers tips, not having the courage to have at least given it a try.

Don't open the door for someone else to be in her arms, where you should rightfully be.

When you feel oh so lonely and long for her touch, just quiet yourself and let yourself feel your inner soul reaching out to her.

She is your soul mate, and surely you must know she is your destiny.

There will be a light and a burning deep within your soul, a warming essence of her being.

Let go of any fear, for it is an illusion.

Go towards the light and don't be afraid.

Go towards the love, the peace, the companionship, the happiness, the joy, and the fulfillment.

Go towards a wonderful life, for the rest of your life, for there is no other conclusion.

Stand at the edge of the Grand Canyon, jump in faith knowing you will surely grow wings and fly.

Everything will be all right, everything will be just fine.

Take the word of your angels, her heart is pure and her love is true.

She will not disappoint you; she will not let you down.

You are meant to be together purely, this is God's plan, to this you must resign.

Ask yourself, are you going to fulfill your destiny?

With Love,

Your Angels

Her Fear

Her Fear

Oh the fear, that horrible horrible fear raising its cruel hand of terrible destruction.

Visions of gloom, shadows of doubt, creep into her mind, creating feelings of crushing rejection.

A painful heaviness consumes her mind, in its unmerciful grip she sinks lower and lower into the depths of hell.

Images of illusions growing out of proportion, thoughts of torment relentlessly pulling her into their evil spell.

Her heart is pounding out of control, louder and louder, unrelenting, there is nowhere to run.

Oh, what terrible visions her mind has conjured up, in her made-up creation, what kind of horrible monster has she become?

She desperately tries to gain control; her mind so taut not even the angels can comfort her, oh... if only for God's help she would ask.

Fear, always unyielding in its destruction, a dark essence hiding behind an ugly mask.

Its dark barrier of destructive deception consumes her every thought; immersed in her own self-pity, it suffocates her with its ever-gripping hold so tight.

So powerful, so strong, fear Oh, yes, fear, stealing dreams and destroying lives, leaving no survivors from its horrible might.

Angels watch from the heavens above; their harps are silent... for they know broken hearts are in the creation.

Fear Oh, yes, fear, the destroyer of love, taking away the beautiful, golden rays of the sun, the colorful rainbow of hope, the angels weep and no longer sing in grand elation.

When the brutal winds have settled, she sits down alone, weeping tears of remorse, surrounded by her self-made destruction, she asks, oh, what has she done?

In painful regret, kneeling to pray, she asks God if He can make things right, can all the wrath and destruction created from fear... oh, dear God, can it be undone?

In answer to her prayers, sent by God, three beautiful golden angels, each one descends, touching her soul, comforting her and ridding the horrible torment within her mind.

Confronting fear, her very own private war from within, fear strong and forceful, determined to win, putting her trust in God; there is no doubt this battle she will win.

Oh yes... sweet... sweet... victory, her fear now confined, now inner peace she is able to find.

House of Fine Crystal and Meth

House of Fine Crystal and Meth

Today a woman cries out in agony, trying desperately to hide from an illusionary reality, her soul lost in hopelessness and despair.

Just around the corner, on the other side of the door; where darkness tightly clutches her being, held fast in its relentless grip, she sinks further and further into the profundity of her own deception and fear.

Her human form wrapped in a burning flame, consumed in unmerciful anguish, she runs from anything and everything, unable to escape the horrifying vision of Satan's deep penetrating glare.

Her heart aches for love, to be safe and secure in the warmth of God's loving embrace, to believe that He has not forsaken her, wanting to believe that by her side He is always near.

Drawn to the house of fine crystal and meth, she finds temporary shelter from the destructive winds of her inner storm, silently crying tears of shame and self blame.

She is never heard and never seen, a dealer; in the night silently luring others into her house of crystal and meth, lies and illusions they do not understand.

Her sanctuary in crystal and meth destroyed by the shattering of dreams, left homeless in the cold of the night, facing the suffering of a temporary fix, she cries out in relentless pain.

A lady of the evening, she must pay the price, invisible to love and vulnerable to the evil etchings of virile designs, her life eroding as the desert sand.

Sweet Child of God, living in a house of fine crystal and meth.

Reaching to the heavens she begs to be spared with every breath.

Find me if you will; I'm here, over here, hiding in the corner just behind the door.

Shower your mercy upon me, for I can no longer fight this self-inflicted war.

She sees all her imperfections in an untruthful mirror, not feeling good enough to be who she really is, believing she is not worthy of having what she truly desires.

Oh… this woman who has lost all hope, this woman who thinks she has depraved her soul, if only she could see her truth and her destiny.

She alone can make the decision to emerge from this retched deep, black hole; she alone must find the strength and the courage to put out her inner fires.

There is so much at stake, there is an urgent purpose to her life, a destiny that is carved in stone; the time is now; not one second more can be wasted; it is here and now that she must set herself free.

Many angels stand by her side guiding her to the other side of the door, golden rays of light shine upon her lovely, radiant face.

Pain and anguish left behind, addictions and favors are in her past, joy and happiness reside this side of the door.

A diamond beautifully polished for all to see; an exquisite butterfly has finally found its rightful place.

A woman who has found her truth, a loving woman who has become a beautiful butterfly; in the hearts of many she is loved and in the highest of heaven's realms for all eternity she will soar.

Sweet Child of God, living in a house of fine crystal and meth.

Reaching to the heavens she begs to be spared with every breath.

God found her; He always knew she was there; hiding in the corner just behind the door.

He showered His mercy upon her blessed soul; for now she can hear the fearless lion within her roar.

Sweet Child of God, who once lived in a house of fine crystal and meth.

She found her way from behind the door.

Now she sits amongst a garden of beautiful flowers, surrounded in God's love for ever more.

This woman, who once lived in a house of fine crystal and meth.

About The Author

C. J. Lovell was born in Provo, Utah and grew up just a few miles away in the small town of Orem. While growing up she loved to ride horses, snow ski and write short stories.

She graduated from the University of Arizona Certified Public Managers program. Although her education was focused on Business Administration, her first love was anything that brought out her creative side. C. J. is a world traveler and lived overseas for ten years.

She has worked for a number of years in the computer field as an Information Security Analyst, also doing WEB design part time. Along with her technical expertise, she is a poet, author and artist.

She lives in Phoenix Arizona, with her husband and her cat Angel. She is the mother of two grown sons, has a beautiful daughter-in-law and two adorable grandsons. She also has a grand cat, Hank and a grand dog, Reagan.

For more information about C. J. Lovell or to order books, go to www.cjlovell.com

www.ingramcontent.com/pod-product-compliance
Lightning Source LLC
Chambersburg PA
CBHW030937150426
42812CB00064B/2979/J